Think Quick,

Act Fast:

Navigating Challenges with Speed and Precision"

Copyright Contents

TABLE OF CONTENT

Chapter 1: The Power of Rapid Decision-Making

The capacity to act swiftly and wisely is a crucial quality that can distinguish people and organizations in today's fast-paced world of perpetual change and growing difficulties. In today's dynamic environment, success is largely dependent on the ability to make decisions quickly.

Speed is a must

Why is making decisions quickly so important? The speed of contemporary life is the solution. The rate of change and the speed of information transmission have both increased significantly in both corporate and personal affairs. For instance, technology has completely changed industry, reducing product life cycles and boosting competition. The digital age has increased access to information and options in our daily lives.

In such a situation, procrastination might be expensive. Opportunities might go, issues can worsen, and the drive for advancement can be lost. People with quick decision-making skills have an advantage over others.

A Study of Quick Thinking Psychology

Making decisions quickly includes a complicated interaction of cognition and intuition, not just making fast decisions without thinking. It's the capacity to quickly analyze a problem, balance the available options, and decide a condensed amount of time. It involves having the mental flexibility to efficiently comprehend information.

Psychologists have found several elements that support efficient rapid decision-making, including:

Pattern Recognition: Skilled decision-makers quickly spot patterns in data or circumstances. They can use their abilities to apply pertinent answers and draw from prior experiences.

Intuition: Information is processed subconsciously to produce intuition, which is frequently referred to as a gut feeling. If it's developed via experience and knowledge, it can be a potent instrument for making quick decisions.

Information Filtering: Quick decision-makers are adept at eliminating unimportant information and concentrating on the most important elements.

Risk assessment: They are skilled at quickly weighing rewards and risks, which enables them to make decisions even in ambiguous situations.

Decision-Making Heuristics: Their Function

Heuristics are mental shortcuts or general principles that we employ to streamline difficult decision-making processes. They have some limitations but can be useful for making hasty decisions. Typical heuristics for making decisions include:

Availability Heuristics: These include making decisions based on information that is easily accessible. We might overestimate the likelihood of a risk if recent news stories have highlighted it. We frequently base our decisions on the first piece of information we come across, which is known as the "anchoring heuristic." If the starting information is incorrect, this may result in biases.

Confirmation bias is the tendency for people to seek out information that supports their own opinions or choices, which results in biased judgment.

Heuristics can speed up decision-making, but if used carelessly, they can also result in mistakes. When necessary, good decision-makers strike a balance between the use of heuristics and analytical reasoning

The Effect on Business

The ability to act quickly can make or ruin a company in the corporate world. Imagine a situation when a business encounters unanticipated market turbulence. Competitors who can analyze the situation swiftly, modify their plans, and exploit chances as they arise can have a major advantage over those who hesitate or respond slowly.

Particularly startups benefit from making decisions quickly. Many startups use lean and agile approaches, which emphasize rapid iterations, learning from mistakes, and real-time adaptation. With this strategy, they can change course as needed to maintain their lead in fiercely competitive marketplaces.

Obstacles and Challenges: Rapid decision-making has indisputable power, but it's not without difficulties and dangers. Typical challenges include:

Overconfidence: People who make conclusions quickly may occasionally become overconfident and think their judgments are inflatable.

The capacity to act swiftly and wisely is a crucial quality that can distinguish people and organizations in today's fast-paced world of perpetual change and growing difficulties. In today's dynamic environment, success is largely dependent on the ability to make decisions quickly.

Lack of Information: In some instances, the haste to decide may cause important information to be missed.

Decision Fatigue: Constantly making snap decisions can cause mental tiredness and eventually cause choices to be of lower quality.

Organizations with a culture that favors deliberate, delayed decision-making may be resistant to efforts to adopt quick decision-making.

In Chapter 2, we'll go more deeply into methods for honing the ability to think quickly and look at solutions to these problems. In the interim, keep in mind that making decisions quickly is not only about speed; it's also about having the ability to make wise decisions in a world that is changing quickly. In some instances, the haste to decide may cause important information to be missed.

Chapter 2: Strategies for Quick Thinking

The capacity to think rapidly and make quick judgments is a vital advantage in today's fast-paced environment. Having a set of rapid thinking skills may make a major difference whether faced with a vital corporate choice, a personal difficulty, or just navigating the intricacies of daily life. In this chapter, we'll look at numerous tactics and ways to improve your rapid thinking.

1. Accept Mental Preparedness

Maintaining a condition of mental preparation is one of the most important tactics for rapid thinking. This entails being mentally flexible and prepared to adapt to unforeseen events. This is how you can do it:

Stay Informed: Stay current on pertinent information in your career or area of interest. When faced with fresh issues, this knowledge base will serve as a basis for fast thinking.

Mental Workouts: Perform mental workouts and puzzles that need quick problem-solving. Sudoku, crossword puzzles, and brain teasers are all great ways to keep your mind alert.

Mental Scenario Planning: Experiment with mental scenario planning. Consider hypothetical circumstances and how you might react to them. This mental practice may help you respond more quickly in comparable circumstances in real life.

2 Develop Analytical Thinking

Quick thinking does not imply rash, unwise conclusions. It requires the capacity to quickly assess events and make appropriate decisions.

Here are some methods for developing analytical thinking:

Develop critical thinking abilities through challenging assumptions, assessing evidence, and considering different viewpoints. This will allow you to make speedy, well-informed judgments.

Use decision trees or flowcharts to lay out potential outcomes and choices. This visual tool may assist you in swiftly navigating complicated options.

3. SWOT Analysis: Use SWOT (Strengths, Weaknesses, Opportunities, Threats) analysis to evaluate problems from several perspectives and determine the best course of action.

Use Your Intuition: Intuition, often known as gut feeling, may be a useful tool for rapid thinking. It's the outcome of your subconscious brain digesting information quickly. To successfully use your intuition.

Pay Attention to Your Gut Responses: Pay attention to your early gut responses in specific circumstances. Your intuition may frequently give useful information.

4. Practice Intuitive Decision-Making: Make tiny judgments based on your gut instinct to strengthen your intuition. You'll get more sensitive to it with time.

check Your Intuition: When feasible, check your intuitive conclusions with evidence or logical reasoning to guarantee they are accurate.

5. Maintain Your Cool Under Pressure

In high-pressure circumstances, quick thinking is often put to the test. It is critical to be able to stay cool and collected. Here's how to keep your cool:

Deep Breathing: Deep breathing methods might help you manage stress and anxiety. In stressful situations, taking deep breaths might help you restore concentration and clarity.

Pause and Reflect: Before making a choice, take a minute to pause and reflect, particularly in high-pressure circumstances. This quick pause may help you avoid making rash decisions.

Mental Resilience: Build mental resilience by subjecting oneself to difficult experiences or controlled pressures. You'll gradually get more at ease making judgments under duress.

6. Establish Effective Time Management

When it comes to rapid thinking, time is sometimes a precious resource. Effective time management may assist you in allocating resources wisely:

Prioritization entails identifying the most important activities or choices and addressing them first. This keeps you from becoming bogged down in trivial concerns.

Establish Time restrictions: Set time restrictions for decision-making. This limitation may push you to concentrate on the important and avoid overthinking.

Delegate When Appropriate: Delegate certain activities or choices to those who are better qualified to manage them if feasible. Delegation may free up your time for more important tasks.

Adaptation and Continuous Learning

Quick thinking is a talent that can be honed and polished with practice. It is critical to have an attitude of continual learning and adaptation:

Experience teaches: Consider your previous choices and their results. Use these experiences to help you make better decisions in the future.

Seek input from reliable coworkers, mentors, or friends. They might provide useful information about your decision-making style and places for growth.

alter to Change: Be flexible and alter your methods as necessary. The world is continuously changing, and so should your fast-thinking techniques.

7. Run Decision-Making Simulations

Simulate decision-making situations to improve and hone your rapid thinking abilities. This may be accomplished in a variety of ways, including:

Role-Playing: Participate in role-playing activities in which you assume various roles and make judgments depending on the circumstances.

Create realistic situations relevant to your career or life and practice making choices under time limits.

Mentorship: Seek advice from someone who has shown rapid thinking, such as emergency responders or successful entrepreneurs. They may provide significant insights and advice.

Improve Your Communication Skills

Effective communication is often linked to rapid thinking, particularly in collaborative settings. Improve your communication abilities by doing the following:

Active Listening: Use active listening to ensure that you completely comprehend the facts and views provided during a discussion.

Clarity and Conciseness: Learn to communicate your thoughts and conclusions clearly and succinctly. Avoid using jargon or being too verbose.

Create a feedback loop in your communication to guarantee that messages are received and comprehended correctly.

9. Adopt Technology

Technology may be a great ally in rapid thinking in today's digital age:

Information Access: Make use of technology to get quick access to information. Search engines, databases, and research tools may instantly give you the information you need.

Apps and Tools: Look into apps and software that may help with decision-making, project management, and time management.

Automate repetitive tasks to free up mental energy for critical thinking.

10. Seek Diverse Points of View

Seeking out other ideas and engaging with others may help to improve quick thinking.

Brainstorming: Hold brainstorming meetings with colleagues or friends to swiftly explore alternative solutions and ideas.

Diversity of Thought: Surround yourself with people from various backgrounds and points of view. They may provide new perspectives that you may not have considered.

Consult professionals: In complicated or specialized sectors, seek the advice of professionals who have specialized knowledge and experience.

Incorporating these rapid thinking skills into your everyday life may result in better decision-making and a stronger capacity to manage problems with speed and accuracy. Keep in mind that rapid thinking is a talent that can be acquired and perfected through time, and practice is essential for mastery. In the next chapter, we'll look at real-world implementations of these tactics and how they might be used in certain situations.

Chapter 3: Navigating Ambiguity with Precision

The capacity to negotiate ambiguity with precision is a talent that may set people and organizations apart in a world marked by rapid change and complexity. When there is a lack of clarity or knowledge, ambiguity frequently emerges, making decision-making difficult. This chapter will look at tactics and approaches for dealing with uncertainty and making accurate judgments.

Recognizing Ambiguity

Ambiguity may appear in a variety of ways:

Information Gaps: When critical information is missing or incomplete, making educated judgments becomes challenging.

Uncertainty may be caused by conflicting facts or contradicting knowledge.

Ambiguity may also occur in very complicated circumstances with various variables and causes at play.

Uncertain Outcomes: Ambiguity exists when the result of a choice is uncertain or the implications are unclear.

Precision Is Everything

Navigating ambiguity is about making precise judgments that correspond with your aims and beliefs, not merely making decisions in the face of uncertainty. Precision in decision-making entails making well-informed, carefully thought, and context-specific decisions.

Precision Strategies for Navigating Ambiguity

Obtain Extensive Information

Gathering as much information as possible is the first step in managing uncertainty. This includes the following:

Conducted extensive investigation to address knowledge gaps. Use credible sources and, where required, seek the advice of specialists.

Data Collection: Gather pertinent information about the problem. Surveys, interviews, or data analysis may be used.

Scenario Analysis: Think about numerous situations and their possible consequences. This helps you anticipate many scenarios.

Accept Adaptive Thinking

Ambiguity often necessitates adaptable and agile thinking. Avoid one-size-fits-all solutions and be willing to change your strategy when new information becomes available.

Scenario Planning: Create contingency plans for various circumstances. This enables you to easily pivot if the circumstance changes.

Iterative Decision-Making: Make incremental choices, reviewing and changing them as new information becomes available.

Seek for Different Points of View

Diverse views may bring significant insights and alternate ideas when confronted with uncertainty. This allows you to look at the problem from several perspectives and make better-informed conclusions.

Collaborate with colleagues, specialists, or mentors who can provide fresh insights and knowledge.

Cross-functional Teams: To address difficult challenges, form cross-functional teams. Each team member brings a unique skill set and point of view to the table.

Make use of Decision-Making Frameworks

Frameworks for decision-making provide systematic techniques for dealing with ambiguity:

Cost-Benefit Analysis: Determine the costs and advantages of various choices. This might assist you in making choices that are in line with your objectives.

Lists of Pros and Cons: Make a list of the advantages and disadvantages of each choice. This visual tool might help you make better decisions.

Decision Trees: Use decision trees to sketch out various choice routes and consequences

Effective Risk Management

Ambiguity is often associated with danger. Risk management is critical for making accurate decisions:

Risk Evaluation: Determine the degree of risk associated with each choice. Consider the likelihood and possible consequences of various events.

Risk Mitigation: Create measures to reduce possible hazards. This might include contingency preparations or risk-reduction strategies.

Establish Specific Goals

It is critical to have defined objectives and goals to make accurate decisions:

Goals should be Specific, Measurable, Achievable, Relevant, and Time-bound (SMART). This insight might help you make decisions.

Prioritization: Determine which goals are most important in the present situation.

Make use of technology and data analytics.

Technology and data analytics may give significant insights for resolving uncertainty in today's data-driven world:

Big Data Analytics: Use big data analytics to find patterns and trends that may not be obvious at first.

Predictive Analytics: Using current data, predictive modeling may assist in estimating probable consequences.

Implement decision support systems that make suggestions based on algorithms and data analysis

Control Cognitive Biases

Cognitive biases may impair judgment and lead to poor judgments. Recognize and minimize typical biases such as confirmation bias and anchoring bias.

Develop critical thinking skills to question assumptions and avoid cognitive traps.

Peer Review: Seek feedback from others to help you overcome personal prejudices and blind spots.

Accept Ambiguity as a Possibility

Instead of seeing uncertainty as a hindrance, consider it an opportunity for invention and creativity:

Ambiguity often necessitates imaginative problem-solving. Investigate novel solutions that may not have been explored in a more specific setting.

Learning Opportunity: Accept uncertainty as an opportunity to learn and develop. Each uncertain circumstance teaches us something about future decision-making.

Use Ethical Decision-Making

It is important to make judgments that are consistent with ethical beliefs and ideals while dealing with ambiguity:

Consider the ethical ramifications of your actions and make sure they line with your moral compass.

Maintain transparency in your decision-making process, particularly when dealing with uncertainty. Explain your reasoning and aims clearly.

Real-Life Applications

Consider the following real-world example to demonstrate the tactics for handling ambiguity with precision:

A firm is thinking of entering a new market with a disruptive product. However, market circumstances are unpredictable, and data are scarce. While developing a detailed market entrance plan, decision-makers must negotiate ambiguity.

Strategy Implementation:

Gather as much information as possible by doing market research, competitive analysis, and consumer surveys.

Adopt Adaptive Thinking: Create a flexible market entrance strategy that can be altered in response to changing market circumstances.

Seek varied Perspectives: To give varied perspectives, form a cross-functional team with individuals from marketing, sales, and finance.

Use Decision-Making Frameworks: Conduct a cost-benefit analysis to assess the possible risks and benefits of joining the market.

Risk Management: Create contingency plans for all circumstances, including unanticipated market downturns.

Set Specific Goals: Establish specific market entrance goals, such as market share targets and revenue targets.

Predictive analytics and technology may be used to anticipate market trends and customer behavior.

Be cautious of confirmation bias, which may encourage decision-makers to interpret limited facts in ways that reinforce their prior ideas.

Embrace Ambiguity as an Opportunity: Encourage creative thinking among team members to investigate unorthodox market entrance methods.

Ethical Decision-Making: Ensure that the company's market entrance plan matches its ethical ideals, while also respecting local conventions and legislation

Using these tactics, decision-makers may manage the uncertainty of market entrance while making precise and informed judgments that are consistent with the company's aims and beliefs.

Conclusion

In today's complicated and fast-changing environment, the ability to navigate ambiguity with accuracy is crucial. By combining data collection, adaptive thinking, varied views, and decision-making frameworks,

Chapter 4: Leading Through Swift Action

The capacity to lead via fast action is often the characteristic of a successful and powerful leader in the realm of leadership. Leaders who can think fast and make rapid judgments have a big influence on their businesses and teams. In this chapter, we will look at the necessity of quick action and the tactics that leaders may use to do so successfully.

The Importance of Quick Action in Leadership

Leadership entails directing an organization or a group of people toward a shared purpose or vision. Leaders must be prepared to make quick choices to solve difficulties, exploit opportunities, and adapt to changing circumstances in a quickly changing environment. Here are some of the main reasons why quick response is critical in leadership:

Competitive edge: The capacity to adapt swiftly to market changes, client needs, and new trends may give a major competitive edge in highly competitive sectors.

Leaders must make quick judgments during crises or emergencies to safeguard the safety and well-being of their employees and stakeholders.

Leaders must build an agile and speedy decision-making culture to support innovation and respond to new technology or market disruptions.

staff Engagement: Showing that leaders are proactive and attentive to problems and recommendations helps enhance staff morale and engagement.

To accomplish corporate objectives, leaders must allocate resources effectively and make timely choices on funding, staffing, and project priorities.

Quick Action Strategies for Leadership

Decisiveness and Vision Clarity

Effective leaders have a clear vision and a thorough knowledge of the objectives of their firm. Because they understand how each option fits into the overall goal, they can make judgments quickly. To improve decisiveness:

Prioritize objectives: To offer direction and context for decision-making, clearly prioritize short-term and long-term objectives.

Communicate the Vision: Make certain that your team knows the organization's vision, purpose, and values so that their actions are consistent with it.

Delegate Authority: Give team members the authority to make choices in their areas of competence, minimizing the need for hierarchical approvals.

Data-Informed Decision-Making

Data is a great tool for making educated decisions. Leaders who depend on data may make more timely and accurate judgments. To properly exploit data:

Collect Relevant Data: Identify key performance indicators (KPIs) and collect data that is relevant to the aims of your firm.

Develop the capacity to interpret data quickly, employing analytics tools and software as required.

Delegate Data Analysis: Assign data analysis duties to individuals on your team who are experts in data-driven insights.

Risk Evaluation and Management

Rapid action often entails considering and managing the risks involved with a choice. Leaders must be capable of spotting possible hazards and successfully managing them.

Risk Assessment: Before making major choices, do rigorous risk assessments. Consider the likelihood and magnitude of possible dangers.

Risk Tolerance: Define and convey the organization's risk tolerance to the team. This facilitates the alignment of risk-taking behaviors with company objectives.

Contingency Planning: Create contingency plans for high-risk actions, including what measures to follow in the event of a negative result.

Effective communication

Communication is essential for quick action. Leaders must communicate choices properly and ensure that their people understand why those decisions were made.

Timely communication is essential for avoiding misunderstanding and ambiguity among team members.

Transparency: Be open and honest about your decision-making process and the reasons you examine when making decisions.

Encourage team members to express their opinions and concerns, and actively listen to their responses.

Adaptability and agility

Leaders must embrace change and be adaptive to changing conditions. A critical leadership characteristic is the ability to pivot rapidly when required.

Consider using agile processes, which stress iterative, adaptable approaches to project management and issue solutions.

Continuous Learning: Encourage team members to adapt to new knowledge and insights by cultivating a culture of continuous learning and progress.

Scenarios: Create scenarios for future changes or obstacles and prepare answers ahead of time.

Team Empowerment

Effective leaders understand that they cannot make all choices on their own. They delegate decision-making authority to their teams within their areas of responsibility.

Delegation: Give team members decision-making power based on their skills and knowledge.

Training and Development: Invest in team members' training and development to improve their decision-making abilities.

Build trust within the team while holding team members responsible for their choices and actions.

Prioritization and Time Management

Leaders are often faced with a plethora of jobs and choices. Effective time management and prioritizing are required to guarantee that the most important choices are handled as soon as possible.

Prioritize work: Use strategies such as the Eisenhower Matrix to divide work into urgent and essential categories, enabling you to concentrate on what is most important.

Time Blocking: Set aside specified periods for decision-making and prevent distractions during those times.

Avoid Procrastination: Overcoming procrastination is essential for taking action quickly. Determine your procrastination causes and attempt to reduce them.

Case Study: Taking Quick Action to Lead

Consider the following case study to demonstrate the tactics for leadership via fast action:

Scenario: A major spike in customer complaints regarding late delivery and product quality concerns has been reported by an e-commerce firm. Jane, the CEO, must solve this problem quickly to protect the company's image and customer pleasure.

Strategy Implementation:

Decisiveness and Vision Clarity:

Jane reaffirms the company's commitment to providing excellent customer service and defines the company's objective of being a customer-centric business.

Decision-Making Based on Data:

She examines consumer feedback data to determine the most prevalent problems and their underlying causes.

Risk Evaluation and Management:

Jane evaluates the risks connected with prospective solutions such as supply chain modifications or product quality control.

Communication that works:

She informs her leadership team of the results, establishing clear expectations for changes and a deadline for action.

Adaptability and agility:

Jane forms a cross-functional team charged with quickly making changes and regularly assessing progress.

Team Empowerment:

She let the team take charge of making decisions on improving processes and customer service.

Prioritization and time management:

Jane devotes concentrated attention to overseeing change implementation and allocating appropriate resources.

Jane and her team effectively addressed customer concerns through quick action and the implementation of leadership tactics, resulting in better delivery times and product quality. This shows the company's commitment to excellent customer service and restores consumer confidence.

Conclusion

Rapid action is a dynamic and necessary part of good leadership. Leaders with the ability to think fast, make educated judgments, and act rapidly have a significant effect on their businesses and teams. Leaders can overcome obstacles and seize opportunities by being decisive, using data to make decisions, assessing risks, communicating effectively, being flexible, empowering their team, and managing their time. Quick leadership action.

Chapter 5: Adapting to Change with Agility

Individuals and organizations alike must be able to adapt to change with agility in today's fast-changing environment. Change is unavoidable, whether it comes in the shape of technical advances, market upheavals, or unanticipated disruptions such as the worldwide pandemic. This chapter discusses the significance of responding to change with agility and offers ways for successfully accepting change in both personal and professional settings.

The Characteristics of Change

Change is an unavoidable component of life, and it takes many forms:

Rapid technological advancements change businesses and occupational responsibilities regularly.

Economic circumstances, client tastes, and market trends may all change quickly, affecting companies and sectors.

Natural catastrophes, pandemics, and political upheavals may all have far-reaching consequences for society and the economy.

Personal Transitions: People go through personal transitions such as job changes, relocations, and life milestones.

The Importance of Agility in Change Adaptation

Adapting to change with agility is being able to react swiftly and effectively to changing situations. Individuals and organizations may use it to:

Stay Competitive: Those who can adjust to market fluctuations and client demands get a competitive advantage in business

Decrease Disruption: Quick reactions to disruptions decrease the negative consequences of unexpected occurrences.

Encourage Innovation: An agile strategy stimulates creativity and problem-solving.

Improve Resilience: The capacity to adapt increases resilience, allowing people and organizations to recover from setbacks.

Personal Development: Accepting change promotes personal growth and development.

Agility Strategies for Adapting to Change

Create a Growth Mindset

According to psychologist Carol Dweck, a growth mindset is the concept that talents and intellect can be increased through devotion and hard effort. This mentality is essential for adjusting to change quickly:

Accept Change: View change and difficulties as opportunities for progress rather than threats.

Continuous Learning: Develop a habit of lifelong learning. Proactively seek out new information and abilities.

Persist Despite Setbacks: Failures and setbacks should not discourage you. Consider them as learning opportunities.

Stay Informed and Prepare for Change

Individuals and organizations who are proactive are better positioned to adapt to change. Here's how to efficiently keep informed and anticipate change:

Continuously examine your surroundings for indicators of change, whether in your business or your personal life.

Market Research: Conduct market research in a corporate setting to identify consumer patterns and upcoming technology.

Scenarios: Create scenarios for potential future changes and prepare actions appropriately.

Develop Your Adaptability Skills

Specific abilities may improve adaptability

Problem-Solving: Sharpen your problem-solving abilities to successfully face issues.

Develop emotional intelligence to regulate your own emotions and negotiate interpersonal interactions during times of transition.

Resilience: Improve your resilience to recover from hardship and failures.

Effective communication

Communication is critical in assisting people through transitions. Effective communication tactics, whether you're a leader or a team member, include

Transparency entails being open and honest about the reasons for the change and its possible consequences.

Active listening entails actively listening to others' problems and comments.

Empathy: Be compassionate toward others who are dealing with change.

Accept Technology and Automation

Technology may help to simplify operations and improve adaptability:

Automation: Use automation to streamline operations and decrease manual activities whenever feasible.

Digital Tools: Especially in distant or virtual work situations, use digital tools and platforms for cooperation and communication.

Create an Adaptability Culture

Creating an adaptive culture in businesses is critical:

Leadership: Leaders should exemplify and promote adaptation in their employees.

Training and Development: Invest in adaptability-promoting training and development programs.

Establish feedback systems for workers to express concerns and recommendations about change.

Create a Support System

Having a support network during times of transition may give emotional support and guidance:

Mentors: Seek advice from mentors or experienced persons who have gone through similar transitions.

Connect with others who are going through similar transitions to exchange experiences and strategies.

Consider expert coaching to help you improve adaptation and resilience.

Real-Life Applications

Let's look at how these tactics may be used in practice:

Scenario: A manufacturing business is experiencing a dramatic change in market demand owing to shifting client preferences for sustainable and environmentally friendly goods.

Strategy Implementation:

Create a Growth Mindset:

Employees are encouraged by the leadership team to consider this transformation as a chance to innovate and build new sustainable goods.

Stay Informed and Prepare for Change:

The organization performs market research regularly to remain ahead of consumer trends and to identify the rising need for eco-friendly goods.

Develop Adaptability Skills:

The company funds training programs to improve problem-solving and emotional intelligence abilities.

Communication that works:

The leadership team conveys the reasons for the move and the company's commitment to sustainability to workers, assuring them of the company's future.

Accept Technology and Automation:

The corporation invests in automation to simplify manufacturing processes for long-lasting goods.

Create an Adaptability Culture:

The leadership team encourages creative ideas for sustainable goods and promotes a welcoming environment that supports adaptation.Create a support system:

Employees can talk to mentors and support groups about challenges and ideas related to the change in demand.

To stay competitive, the manufacturing business responds to market demand, introduces sustainable goods, and employs these tactics..

Conclusion

Agility in adapting to change is not only a vital talent but also a mentality that may contribute to personal and organizational progress. Embracing change helps people succeed in a constantly changing world..Individuals and organizations can navigate change with confidence and resilience by developing a growth mindset, staying informed, cultivating adaptability skills, embracing effective communication, leveraging technology, fostering a culture of adaptability, and building a support network.

www.ingramcontent.com/pod-product-compliance
Lightning Source LLC
Chambersburg PA
CBHW062303290526
45794CB00006B/2677